Paradontic

Paradontic

Poetic, Monologs, and Storytellings, Based on Tales of Love, Faith, Encouragement, and Romance

Jobie Sprout

PARADONTIC

POETIC, MONOLOGS, AND STORYTELLINGS, BASED ON TALES OF LOVE, FAITH, ENCOURAGEMENT, AND ROMANCE

iUniverse books may be ordered through booksellers or by contacting:

iUniverse
1663 Liberty Drive
Bloomington, IN 47403
www.iuniverse.com
844-349-9409

Because of the dynamic nature of the Internet, any web addresses or links contained in this book may have changed since publication and may no longer be valid. The views expressed in this work are solely those of the author and do not necessarily reflect the views of the publisher, and the publisher hereby disclaims any responsibility for them.

Any people depicted in stock imagery provided by Getty Images are models, and such images are being used for illustrative purposes only.
Certain stock imagery © Getty Images.

ISBN: 978-1-5320-5109-8 (sc)
ISBN: 978-1-5320-5110-4 (e)

Library of Congress Control Number: 2018906509

Print information available on the last page.

iUniverse rev. date: 12/29/2020

Contents

Dedication

I am proud to dedicate this book to my late dad, Gerald J. James, and my beloved mom, Neva A. James. To Jah Irving, who always takes the time to support, read, edit, and criticize when needed. To my husband, Gilbert, my daughter, Shanique and her husband, Scott, and my sons, Ricardo and David, and the two new lovely extensions to the family, Samaya and Sando, who understand my absent times in their lives and my love for them.

To my distant husband whose support I had better not need but who can always spare the change if I can cook up a lie for its usage instead of telling him it is for my creativity. I thank you from the bottom of my heart, for without you in my life, who else would I be?

To my friend Brenda at Harvest Production, who is on this writing journey with me. She always takes the time to remind me to write at least a page per day. I truly love and adore Marc Anthony Butcher, a thirty-five-year self-publisher, poet, author, and veteran. He wrote "Poem Promoting Peace" and "Before the Divorce, Read This." One of his titles I like in particular is "When You Love Someone, Really Love Them." Ever since the first day I met him, he has been a great supporter of my work and was the main reason I decided to publish *Paradontic*.

To all my family, friends, readers, and sponsors, I thank you for your continuing loyal love and support.

Most importantly, I thank You, Jehovah God, for trusting me to go through life's trials, temptations, and tribulations. You know me best. I thank you for being the wings beneath my wings during the times, I'm just not able to fly. Jehovah God, You always see me through the storms, even though the anchor of my ship came loose and my ship wrecked way out in the deep blue sea. You haven't let me drown, even though I've been swimming a little bit longer than I'd like. You've been keeping me safe from the sharks. But who says time is on my side? Who is the master timekeeper? My Lord God, "Jehovah Is the Master Time Keeper." "Please Be Still, My Friends"—my God Jehovah is always on time. Throughout our lives, God will never leave our side.

Throughout this book, you'll find no room for haters. Learn how to enjoy life with those you're blessed to have in your life. Families are deserving of your love, first and foremost. I pray that you'll find my storytelling insightful, delightful, and a bit spicy. I love you—that is true, but do know that Jehovah God loves you much more.

1

Love

Love, in my opinion, is very gratifying and unexplainable. However, one thing is for certain: we are all cable of loving because we were born to love, truly. Hate, on the other hand, is, sadly, "thought."

So I would love to dedicate this chapter to all of us who have been loved at some point or have loved someone to the point of forgotten self.

1

Mother Dearest

Dear Mother Dearest,

I woke up in the twilight zone thinking of how radiantly and effortlessly your light glows. I'm so very happy that you are my mommy, my foresight, my insight, my backbone. Courageously, your sparks glisten in your words, in your actions, and in your style. Through life's trials and tribulations, you echo a mightiness that is so impressive. No matter what life throws at you, still you glow.

I pray that should you have to leave this world before I do (as we all might some unknown day), I do hope that all you've instilled in me I'll forever cherished. With the greatest respect, admiration, and gratitude for all that you are and do, I sincerely appreciate having you in my life.

I love you, Mother Dearest.

Your beloved child, by God's grace and mercies.

— 2 —

My Grand mama

My grandmamma Ruby Graford got moves.
Oh! Look at my grandmamma dancing to the rhythm of one of her favorite songs:
Span-spa-na, span-spa-na-na-na-na-na.
In her polka dot skirt, pleated from waist to knee high,
Her hips are swinging from side to side.
Her knees are bopping in between her Turks.
Her box-braided gray hair is flying in the air.
Shaking her skinny legs that are permanently bent,
"Go, Granny, go," the neighborhood kids are shouting.
My grandmamma don't mind the attention, you see.
My grandmamma just keep dancing to
Span-spa-na, span-spa-na-na-na-na-na.

3

Mama Too

Mama Too drops what she's doing to give a mother a helping hand, just so she can put up her feet, take an extra snooze if needed, or just a day with friends away from her daily responsibilities.

Mama Too has to change a diaper or two. Baby sat overnight. Takin' the child to the library and park. Helped me stand while I tried to walk, till at last I could stand up and run.

Mama Too's arms feel no different from my mother's. Her kisses and hugs are filled with love, joy, and pride.

Mama Too, I love and appreciate you. This is why on such a special day I see fit to honor you with the utmost admiration and gratitude.

Sincerely yours.

4

Papa Too

Papa Too understands what it takes to become a better man and lends a helping hand when Dads falls short.

Papa Too may not say too much, but he knows when to give his input. He may not make it to the graduations, but he ensured that you made it through school. He may not have the right connections for the job you have applied for, but he made sure you were qualified for the interview. He is not at the finish line tooting his horn but was at the beginning before the race began.

Papa Too, because of your helping hands, I'm the man I am. So on a special day like this, I choose to thank you, honor you, and show you heartfelt appreciation.

Sincerely yours.

── ❧ 5 ❧ ──
Dear Love

Dear love,

Where did we go wrong? What caused you to leave the nest we built on promises we vowed to keep? I wonder if I've become too old, cold, weary, droopy, or simply outdated for you. I wonder if it's because my face ceases to smile, or does it wear a permanent smile? Tell me if it's because you have to repeat every single word you say to me, or is it my shivery hands and feet? Is it the stripes of my wrinkly skin, or is it that my hair has become too silvery and thin?

Dear love,

Deep down inside, I know that I can't get you off my mind. I'm feeling so drenched and out of place without you by my side. I found comfort in the lonely days going by with my hands on my cheeks, wondering what I could have done differently to let you stay by my side the rest of our lives.

Dear love,

Had I known you would someday leave the space where you had placed yourself, for all the years of your looking very comfortable and cozy to me, I would have paid more attention to you. Maybe dust you off a bit, polish you some, and even move you around every now and then. Maybe I should've even gone as far as to sing to you some lullabies, tell you some bedtime stories, even try some new things these young ones are now doing. I wonder, When you left, what memories of me did you take? Did you even bother to take any of the dust that was caught on you, for a keepsake, for golden years' memories?

Dear love,

My love, my heartbeat, my memories, my forever. The root of my divine tree. How much I love you. I want you to know that I thank God for each and every single day we had with each other. I thank God for all the fruit-bearing trees we were able to brood, according to His will.

How I wish up on a lucky star for you, my love, to come back home to me. Come home, my love. Come home. Come back home to me. For love like ours is "paradontic," invincible, and supreme.

Sincerely yours.

—❖ 6 ❖—

Finder Keeper

Come, my love. Come—be my rescuer.
I'm somewhere in a place where only lovers survive.
If love doesn't find me soon,
I'm afraid I'll be no more.

Should love find me, be assured my heart will behold thee
And nothing in the world will cease my joy.

Should love arrive and find me to be no more,
Rest assured I went to my grave unfulfilled.
My soul lingers still.

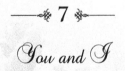

—❖ 7 ❖—

You and I

Two hearts are better than one—
When one gives out,
The other gives in.
You and I together will be
Forevermore.
Each night we kneel down and pray,
Thanking God for

His loving embrace.
You are my partner in life and partner in Christ,
Till death do us part.

8

Love Is True

When you are with the one you love,
You feel no pain—
You feel no shame.
Love's radiance is best seen
Throughout some of the rockiest, most unpredictable times,
When all else's eyes are closed
And silence steals the night.
Lovers share their heartfelt desire,
Wrapped up in emotions, behind closed doors.
Love
Is comforting.
Love …
Is contagious.
Love …
Is colorful.
Love …
Is never ending.
Love …
Is like a flower—when it blooms, it blooms.
Love …
Is truly much more beautiful than you and me.
When love loves you back,
Love …
Is true, true, true.

Like a Rose Garden

A rose is a rose no matter where it's from.
It comes in a variety of colors.
Filled with many thorns.
So are human beings in this earthly garden.
Even though we're from two different worlds,
Just to be your lover,
Like a rose, I will prune away all that I no longer need in my life
So my radiance glows in your eyes.

Make Me Yours

Make me yours, and like lovebirds we'll be flying high—
High above broken bridges,
High above the highest of mountains,
High above the big blue sea, through the stormiest weather.
High above life's uncertainties, together we'll be flying high.

── ❧ 11 ❧ ──

My Darling Sweetheart

Someone must have taken my darling sweetheart from me.

All that's left of us is old-school memories and decades of old-century fashion dos.

Like—I remember when we would walk the streets hand in hand, kissing, kissing.

Oh boy … oh boy, we used to kiss, kiss, and kiss all the time.

Hands could not be kept off each other.

But lately all that has disappeared.

This is the story of my darling sweetheart and me:

Sunday afternoon used to be our flashy walk-the-street day. All dressed up in our best to impress, for the test to tease. Of course, this was what most youngsters still in junior high or high school were doing back then in Jamaica. For economic reasons we stayed in the community instead of going into town, had our parents not opposed. Some people are born smart businessmen and businesswomen. At least our ice cream man was one. For he had mastered our Sunday walks to a tee, knowing the flooded lovers' lane. And *clink-clink, clink-clink* comes he, the ice cream man on his three-wheeler.

My darling sweetheart would buy one Sunday ice cream from his saved-up school lunch money for the week. I myself did the same, to make some contribution, but he was a lady's gentleman, though still in his teens. No way would he have taken any money from me, if he could help it. Our Sunday ice cream had sliced banana, strawberry topping, crushed peanuts, chocolate syrup, and a cherry on top. He would always let me have the cherry if I dared to take it off his tongue. Then, lips over lips and tongue swishing, kind of kissing, would take place a very long time.

Later on, just before it was time to call it a day, a surprise would await me, held in one of his hands behind his back—I had to guess the correct hand. I know you guys are ahead of me and can already guess what came next. Yes, yes, you are so, so right. Something that he could put in his mouth, for more kiss, kiss, kiss. For boy! Oh boy, that baby of mine sure loved to kiss, kiss—lips- and tongue-burning kisses were no game. Mmmm, I'm not sure if it's because that's all we could do and get away with then. Perhaps it was an introduction of who he really was. Who knows, but my baby sure loved to kiss. With a little caressing, if no one was watching. Nipples twitching, legs rubbing a little too close to home. Ah, ah, you very well know what I mean.

Oh well, so much for good parenting, for it didn't work too long for us. Marriage came very quickly to cover up the early pregnancy while our friends were happily off to college. Our romance only got better, though, for we were off living on our own in someone's back room, and we shared an outdoor kitchen and bathroom.

Yes, we kept our romantic love thing going for as long as we could, as a reminder never to part. The kids are all grown up now. The baby is almost out of high school, about to be at his dorm at college. Yeah! I will miss him terribly. My middle one, the only planned-for child, got a little off track, and we are currently working on focusing together, taking it a day at a time. For some strange reason, he and his dad never clicked, but currently both are giving it their best shot. My daughter has her master in medical law. Currently married and the proud mother of two—a boy and a girl.

Something must have happened, though, when the ice cream Sunday vanished. The surprise hand held in the back ceased. The kisses—yes, those very long, lip- and tongue-burning kisses, dropped off this planet earth. It ended, viaduct.

Now I turn to people in search of what to do to get my sweetheart back on track. Some people offer me their condolences, as if he's dead and gone, never coming back. Some offer me their ears, for me to vent. Some save the speeches and give me invitations to their places of worship. Some counsel me all day just to hear themselves talk. Some give me recommendations for online dating sites. Some sincerely love me and feel my pain but just don't know what to say or do.

As for me, I hear only what I want to hear, for no one is going take my sweetheart from me. No way, no how, not if I can help it. So someone please tell me where he could be, for someone must have taken my sweetheart from me.

Enchanted

My life is so divine with you by my side.
I'm intoxicated by your enchanted touch.
We'll be making love in the Atlantic,
No need to be frantic.
Our love will be so magic.
Other lovers will be pedantic.

Should this love ever fade,
Delight would be deleted from my face.
Should this love ever be garnished, love should be banished,
A revolution that would bring Armageddon.

Should this love ever end,
It would be so tragic, just like the *Titanic*.
No need to panic,
Our love is enchanted granted.
No need to stray—
Our love is gigantic; it's paradontic.
You are my organ mechanic,
My generator,
My delighted vine.
You are love itself, granted by God the Almighty.

—❖ 13 ❖—

Stay Away, Haters

Stay away, haters, for I've currently contaminated with the love bug disease.

I have decided to contaminate just one person with it, whoever it may be.

For I'm as sure as I'm certain there is heaven and earth that hatred too shall soon be of the past.

For one person is bound to contaminate another and a vast population is soon to be contaminated with this love bug disease.

So may I please have your permission to contaminate you first?

I promise it won't hurt you any, but it will bring you bounteous peace, joy, and happiness.

—❖ 14 ❖—

Absolutely No Drama, Please

To be my guest, you have to feel
Absolutely
Blessed to be alive,
Absolutely
Positive,
Absolutely
Empathetic,
Absolutely
Caring, giving, and understanding,
Absolutely
Beautifully gorgeous on the inside and out,
Absolutely
Loving, kind, faithful, and true,
Absolutely

Fabulously radiant and bold enough to knock down doors,
Absolutely
Remarkably unbreakable and unstoppable,
Absolutely
Loving of Jehovah God Almighty with your whole heart, mind, and soul.

Yes, it's true—you heard right. You most definitely must love me.
If not, I thank you so very much for crossing yourself off my guest list.
Absolutely yours.

My Head of Gray Hair

My head is full of gray hair—
For sure it is,
But not from the years of wear and tear;
Nor did it grow all in a single day,
But by the grace of God's love, mercy, and infinite wisdom
Cometh today my head of gray hair.

Tradition

This is the house of your great-grandmother.
This is the house your grandma lived in.
This is the house I, your mama, lives in.
This is the house you grew up in.
This is the house you'll live in.
This is the house for your children's children.

2

Faith

I must share with you that these few poems were taken from my many written reminders of my God's amazing ability, love, and grace, in order to cultivate faith when I was just too hurt at the moment to feel His loving embrace.

Whatever faith means to you, it's okay. For me, it is the "trust we have in Jehovah God that all things will be well by the end of the day."

I tell you true that I still today struggle with faith, even after the many miraculous gifts that I've personally received from Jehovah God, through His son, Jesus Christ.

May your faith be rekindled with He who makes all things well.

1

This Faith Thing

Impatience causes frustration.
Frustration causes excruciating pain.
Excruciating pain causes suffering.
Suffering causes consequences.

Consequences can at times cause chronic long-term illnesses.
However, a virtuous person "salvation to him belongs."
So hold on tight to faith, my friends. God is on His way.
I pray that we will all have the faith to practice patience.
Sincerely.

Who Is This God?

I was taught that God is the greatest of all times. A great provider. Master maker of the heavens, the earth, and the entire universe. That He created man and beast to live in peace, unity, and harmony, causing no harm to each other.

Then tell me, please, Why the kitchen hell are some people so damn god-dish mean, self-centered, boastful, hateful, and unbearable? Some are rich, some are poor, some are boorish, some are gifted with talents galore, while others have nothing to claim as their own. Why different shades of color, sizes, heights, hair textures, and all this and that?

Some people live way beyond life's span. Some are stillborn, some are dead before their prime, some linger on and on, just creating a mess for others to deal with even long after they're dead and gone. A life that was supposed to be so grand is now filthier than filth itself.

Some people are living in hope of this paradontic life, where it's said that all will have enough to share. There'll be no crying, no dying, no worries. We'll have regained our close face-to-face connection with God Himself and His son, Jesus Christ. An eternal, perfected life at last.

So who is this God again? The one who has the ability to see all things and knows all things yet sits back and lets things be? No matter what is going on, He has a time for everything. You can mope and cry all you like. He just won't budge until it's the right time.

This God, who causes it to rain on the just and the unjust at the same time. The rich, the poor, the good, and the bad all return to the dust, no matter the cost of their burial.

I truly want to know—who is this God that's not like man? A God who's patient beyond man's comprehension? He who can destroy this world in a second is just shilling. Giving humankind all the time they could ever need for a chance to change their selfish ways.

Look what you have started. You should have never asked me about God had you not the time. For now, I just want to keep going on. This much I know of Him, though: "God has time." Yes! God has time. So the question is, Do we know God's timing?

See—I truly love this God. The one who sent His only begotten son, Jesus Christ, to die for all humankind. That whosoever believes in Him will not perish but have an everlasting paradontic life forevermore. For He will do away with time one faithful, joyous day. So who will need time then?

One thing's for certain: this God of mine is always on time, when you least expect Him. He's like a pregnant lady. No matter the time Mom goes into labor, that baby is sure to come. So come, my loved ones. Waste no more time. Ask the question, Who is this God? I'm just saying. Again and again, He's worth knowing.

3

God Will

God is working on fixing things. Just as he did in the days of Noah, and with Sodom and Gomorrah, so will he replenish this world, again.

I don't know how, but I know God will.

Noah didn't know how, and nor did Lot, but they knew God would.

Neither did Daniel know what God would do while in the lion's pit,

Jonah in the belly of the fish,

Sarah, who gave birth at the age of ninety,

Joseph, who was sold into slavery by his own flesh and blood, then imprisoned by a false witness,

Moses and the big Red Sea,

David and Goliath,

Samson with strength that no man still can comprehend.

We can go on and on, but till we meet again,

Just know that God is able to do all things,

Even though we know not how or when.

We know that somehow He'll make all things well.

Lifeline

There are many gods among us,

Many kings and queens, lords of lords, who are mighty and strong.

However,

There is none mightier than my God, whose name is Jehovah.

His name means "causes to become."

Know that there is nothing that He can't do.

Between you and me, you should give Him a try.

You'll find that He's so fine, merciful, and kind.

As for Me

As for me, Jehovah God Almighty, and Him alone I shall serve, through His son, Jesus Christ.

If anything else, I've learned to take life one day at a time.

Realizing that yesterday is history, today is a mystery,

And tomorrow has its own anxiety.

Now, according to the Bible, we have just been given a one-shot deal at life. So live it well. Enjoy families, friends, and neighbors while you can. Leave, "This world," a better place than you found it. Thus, bring praises to God Almighty.

- ➢ My gift is being healthy.
- ➢ My health is being loving.
- ➢ My love is wealth.
- ➢ My wealth is having freedom of choices.
- ➢ My freedom is the opportunity to live my life to the fullest.

6

My New Year's Prayer

Can someone please tell me when it is New Year's again?
Yes! You're right—what kind of question is this?
See—a New Year for me is each time I have to renew my New Year's wish list.
Though sometimes I feel as if God must be tired of my same old prayer.
For boy, oh boy, I make a mess galore.
For example, on December 31, 2016, just when the clock was about to strike 12 a.m. in 2017
I got down on my knees in Times Square, Manhattan.
There I closed my eyes, holding my head toward the heavens while the confetti blew all over myself and the crowd.
There, I made my promise to God Almighty:

"God, I solemnly swear never again to be the same disobedient, unfaithful, and impatient person."

With all honesty, I meant it, from the bottom of my heart, from my head to my toes.

However, things got the best of me, and New Year came and went, day by day.
But—hoopsy-dooby-doo—my promises I cannot keep.

So here I go again and again, back on my knees in my New York apartment.
New Year three. New Year four, five, six, ten, and maybe one hundred. And it's not even the middle of the year yet. However, here I go again, back down on my knees.

"God, I solemnly swear never again to be the same disobedient, unfaithful, impatient person."

By now I've lost count of how many flipping times I'm going to pray about the same thing.
One thing I know for certain: I am going to achieve my New Year's goal.
One way or the other, with God's grace and mercies.
By the end of this year.
Which ever year it is.

—❦ 7 ❦—

Can I Get an Amen?

Go ahead, you judgers of men, than doers of the words,
Pick up your stones and stone me to death—
Instead of your praises and pray me to health.
As long as no one besides you knows of your secrets tales, not even God,
Go ahead and throw those stones;
Call me all the names in the book,
Like he-she/she-he,
Lady tramp, lady in waiting, lost, broken, or even stolen.
But as far as I know,
No man is perfect; nor is anyone holier than thou.

8

Master Timekeeper

Who says time is on your side?
Who assigned you master timekeeper?
Who determines when it's your turn or mine?
I often dream of when my time comes, how it will feel.
The audience applause, the speech that I would give.
The red carpets and the media press.
The dresses and the many parties.
The moment of truth that I've longed for.
Holding the trophy in both of my hands in fear it might fall.
I wonder, Who will I be mindful to thank, hoping not to forget anyone?
I wonder, Will it be one of the biggest mistakes Hollywood has ever made?
I fear such a dreadful, awful, and terrible mistake.
After all, I've long given up on such a dream ever coming through for me.
But you see—this master timekeeper has nothing to do with your affairs.
Always be prepared, no matter the time of day or how long it may seem to take.
For—make no mistake—God is already there, waiting on time.
Are you on your way to get your price right on time?
It's time for the human race to realize that time is not controlled by humanity.
No one knows the *when* time except our heavenly Father, God Almighty Himself.
He's the Master Timekeeper.
Not you. Not me. Not your friends. Not your neighbors. Not your mama. Not your papa.
So hang in there. Time is on your side, if you are prepared—
Says the Master Timekeeper. Him, not I.

Checkpoint

Faith is not up for sale; nor is it for free.

Faith is your personality imbedded into your soul, mind, and spirit.

So what is your soul, mind, and spirit?

Soul: The opposite of death. A life force in the body that separates the living and the dead (Genesis 2:7).

Mind: The home of wisdom, knowledge, and understanding. The mind is always at work, so use it wisely (1 Corinthians 2:16).

Spirit: The life force of all living things. A gift of light to humankind, who chooses to do God's will (Job 32:8, Proverbs 20:2, Romans 8:16, Ecclesiastes 12:7, 1 Corinthians 6:17).

You've heard the saying "If you can dream it, see it, then you can believe it, and if you believe it, then you can achieve it." How about that for a start?

See—"I believe I can fly." Do you believe that you can fly?

Oh well, don't take my word for it. Just listen to the choir. These people at some point in their once-upon-a-la-la-land lives had to believe that they could fly. This is why they are now flying high, right before our eyes.

Dr. Martin Luther King Jr., Nelson Mandela, Marcus Garvey, T. D. Jakes, Joel Osteen, Noel Jones, TBN TV stations, Michael Phelps, President Barrack Obama, President Donald Trump, First Lady and Secretary of State Hillary Clinton, Simon Fuller, Larry Page and Sergey Brin, Tiger Woods, Usain Bolt, Muhammad Ali, Dr. Ben Carson, Michael Jordan, Steve Jobs, Bill Gates, Mark Zuckerberg, Jack Dorsey, Noah Glass, Evan Williams, J. K. Rowling, Steve Harvey, Bob Marley, Maya Angelou, Oprah Winfrey, Tyler Perry, James Cameron, Dolly Parton, Whitney Houston, Michael Jackson, and my mother, Neva James, did it—and the list goes on and on. Shanique, Ricardo, David, Gilbert, and I, Jobie Sprout, are doing it. Marc Anthony Butcher, Brenda

Lee Gerold, Debra Liverman, and Valdorean Long are doing it. How about you or anyone you know?

So yes! Pray a little, dream a little, play a little, laugh a little, and even cry. But! The Bible says that *works* without faith is dead and *faith* without works is dead.

So get up off your lazy hei-nie and go learn how to fly.

Should you fall and break your wings, "Don't sweat it, my friend." God is beneath those wings.

"I know, for God is carrying me right now,
till my wing is ready to fly again."

10

Friendly Scriptures

Philippians 4:13
John 3:16
Romance 8:6
Joshua 1:18
Proverbs 3:5–5 / Proverbs 18:10
Psalm 23 / Psalm 100
1 Chronicles 22:13
And many more. Please take the time to
invest in a Bible, and read on.

3

Encouragement

This page I dedicate to myself, for all painful life lessons learned and still learning. To my children, who are on this rocky road with me, and all my lovely friends, who have said, "Jobie, thank you for keeping it real." I hope you too will be encouraged, and I know it's never too late to change one's ways. Let's work together, on becoming our better best being. Committed to never stop until our good get gets better, and our better gets best.

1

You Can!

So! Never got to be all that you wanted to be?

Well, haven't you wasted enough time not being all that you can be?

Then can't you spend the same amount of time
To try being what you want to be?

Stop bugging, man,
And use your time wisely
To be all that you can surely be.

2

I Choose

I wonder if I had to choose
Between seeing and hearing,
Between touch and smell,
Between hands and feet,
Families and friends,
Human beings and animals,
Males and females,
Race and color;
Between night and day,
Sun and rain,
Fire and water,
Storms and earthquakes,
Long-term illnesses and poverty;
Between the future and the past;
Between you and me?
See—even though I was not given a choice to be born as me,
I still get to choose. So I choose to be the best that I can be.

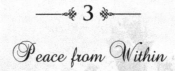

3

Peace from Within

For peace from within, one must change his or her perceptions, priorities, and principles. Always praying to have a forgiving spirit. A pure soul. A loving heart. Be tenderly affectionate. Have a healthy, wealthy, wise mind, spirit, and soul. Have eyes that see nothing but the goodness of others. Have listening ears to hear what people have to say. Have a discerning spirit of understanding. Have the knowledge to delegate compassionately.

    Peace from within can also be cultivated when, once in a while, biannually or annually, you clean your house from top to bottom, as if you were about to relocate to a brand-new house or state, throwing out all unnecessary, long-untouched junk that is cluttering its place of hiding. "For one man's junk is another man's treasure."

Also, every once in a while, rearrange your closets. You can do this by occasion, time of day, season, colors. However, if you find that there's no more space in your closets and you feel as if you want to scream, then go ahead and scream as much as you please. Then it's donating time. Share the love with someone in need or for a worthy cause. Make sure it's something that you would wear or use had you been in their position.

Here is a suggestion for peace from within: time to cook up a fiesta. Invite some neighbors, friends, long-distant relatives you don't get to see unless it's a funeral or wedding, some unpopular coworkers and their loved ones, and some irregular quiet ones from your place of worship. Play some music, and it's time to party!

I'm certain that you can think of so many more ways to peace from within. Anyway, just add mine to your list. If not already activated, time to tap in. I would love to hear from you. "I pray for you and your loved ones to find peace from within." Be blessed, children of God. I love you, but know that God loves you more.

4

Follow Through

Be faithful, graciously.
Be true, honestly.
Be kind, generously.
Be humble, steadfastly.
Be wise, knowingly.
Be loving, ethically.
Be *you*, unapologetically.
Trust in God the Almighty.
And
Follow through … on being you.

5

What Do I Wish?

I wish that I was one of the brightest morning stars,
Way up high, above the big blue sky,
Looking down on your lousy behind,
For you have not taken the time to see that I shine.

I wish that I had a magic wand to switch places with you.
Then you'll know just how much it hurt, by the things you do and say.
How I wish, while I'm sleeping, Prince Charming comes to steal me away,
In hopes that you would've learned to appreciate me more.

6

How Do I Escape the Enemies When It's My Own Family?

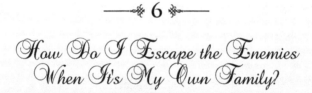

Aren't you my family man
Who's supposed to take good care of me,
Love me,
Guide me,
Protect me,
Feed me if I'm hungry,
Clothe me if I'm naked,
Shelter me from the storms,
Speak words of wisdom when I stray,
Help me to stand should I fall?

So how do I stand a chance of being a better me
When you took advantage of me, making no apologies,

Living in your fantasies?
Now come the hypocrites, pretending to be my outcome,
For what they should've done,
Trying to reshape my mind, which is way overdue.

Now, someone tell me, please!
How do I escape the enemies when it's my own family?
Man! I'm so doggie mad cuz my family I cannot stand.

Exempt

Fade in.

Excuse me!
Ex-cu-se … me!
What did you just say? Why would you want to apologize to a stubborn, rigid fool like me?
Cut, cut!

Quiet on the set, please!
One …
Two …
Three …
Camera rolling—
Take one!
"Action!"

You, listen up and listen well.
I only love you because God says I must love my neighbors as myself.
However, you need to understand that I don't like you one penny—and that's a fact.
You are only in my existence because of my ignorance.

Till at last my intellect shall be regained, you'll be *exempt* from my reality.

Yes, it's true. I do know of your international popularity and that you have friends galore from all walks of life, with the same insane mentality. At the same time, though, I'm so glad that I'm no longer considered one of your friends.

You can trust me on this. There's nothing I'll miss, for this too shall pass, and you owe me no apologies.
For you are *exempt* from my reality, which will prove my integrity and sanity.

8

Rat Race

How bountiful fools—
Those who team up to compete in a heat where there's no track,
Just to beat their prey.
Should you find yourself in such a rat race,
Please stand back.
Give a head start
To the rat racers,
Not to impress
But to protest.
Wait for the result—
You'll find
They false start and are disqualify, thus are unable to finish the race.

9

Red, Not Reddish

My favorite color is red.
Red, I say.
Noooooooooooo, I said red!
Please, please, for goodness' sake, take that reddish
("What it's not") thing back.
You do know that my favorite color is red.
Red,
Red,
Red!
Not reddish, thank you very much.

10

Be You ... Not Me

It isn't easy being me, you know.
So why are you trying so damn hard being me and not you?
It would be best for you to ask me a thing or two. Like, How is it
being me?
And I would reply, "Effortlessly."
However, if you won't regress, then be my guest and waste your precious
time.
For all I can do now is pray that you'll realize how "effortlessly"
It is to be you and not me.

11

Whisperers

Hey, you!
Quit whispering in my ear—
Whisperers of lies,
Scolding tongue,
And chattering tales.
They will find listening ears
From all walks of life
To echo their jealous pains of fares.
Most of the time, on one they may grudge and do not know;
Thus birth gossips in the air,
Which travels near and far
From one whisperer to another, nationwide,
Hence robbing innocent prey of their pride,
Leaving them scarred, sometimes their entire lives.
Now …
There is a call for action
Nationwide
To stop!
Whisperers from
Whispering Lies in
Listeners ears.

—✤ 12 ✤—

No ... Sire

(*Jamaican talking*)

So wait dey!
Yu and mi, nuh di same human beings?
At least that's what they taught me, from way back when, in basic school—
That out of many we are one.

Now you must not spare the rod and spoil the child.
So mi ah go tech mi little time to discipline some
Foolish humankind that have lost their minds.

Mi sey—yu bitcccchhhhh you.
Ah some ah wi dark-skin people ah meck other shades of color—
Red, yellow, black, and white,
Laughing at us.

Caz some of us ah grown like sey
these people's shit nuh stink too.

So answer me this question, please.
Ah nuh the same Master God, weh meck them, meck us to?

Cut the cutlass and have some sense, and first learn to love yourself,
For when we die, it's the same place all human beings will be going—
Right back to the dirt, heaven or hell,
Regardless of ethnicity, nationality, and creed.

So, for goodness' sake, can't all human beings just get along?
"After all, we are Jehovah God, beautiful, beautiful garden."

⸻ ❧ 13 ❧ ⸻

Haste Makes Waste

Focus, focus, Marcus Lucious—
Focus you must,
For haste makes waste.
Don't ask me why;
Just wait you must.
Take time to appreciate life and all that's in it.
Then, when at last you receive your blessings,
Let me be the first you call to share it with.
Aha, aha!
I'm loving it, Marcus Lucious.
Waiting,
That is.

⸻ ❧ 14 ❧ ⸻

Wisdom

I've finally come to an age in my life to realize that I've maximized *stupidity*.
Now, if there is such a word as *stupidity*, then there must be a word as *sensibility*.
Hence, how do I differentiate the two?
First, let's establish their meaning.

Stupidity: Stay stuck in the past over some silly stuff that can't be undone.
This causes a great deal of shame, pain, harm, guilt, and regret.
Sensibility: Realizing that no matter how much we would love to undo the past, that's a task no man can surpass. Therefore, we pick up the pieces, where we left off, and learn how to last.
So now that you've eaten from the Tree of Life, my friend, knowing right from wrong and having acquired wisdom, knowledge, and understanding, wipe your teardrops and quit being a jackass and learn how to *ride an ass*.

❈ 15 ❈

Remember These Proverbs

➤ Silver and gold will vanish away, but a good education will never decay.

➤ Good, better, best—never let it rest till your good gets better and your better gets best.

➤ If at first you don't succeed, try, try, and try again.

➤ Works without faith is dead, and faith without works is dead.

➤ No man is an island. No man stands alone. Each man needs a brother. Each man needs a friend.

➤ Keep knocking, and it shall be open. Keep asking, and it shall be given. Keep seeking, and you shall find.

➤ Better it is to give than to receive.

➤ Forgive—forgive up to "seventy times seven times."

➤ Obey God rather than humankind.

➤ Obey your father and mother, which is the first commandment.

➤ Love thy neighbor as thyself.

➤ Do unto others as you would have them do unto you.

➤ If you pet a dog, it will lick your face, but if you step on that same dog, it will bite you.

The list goes on and on. Please add yours.

— 16 —

A Sales Pitch

I'm knocking on so many no doors just to get to some yes doors.
If today no sales I make,
Tomorrow I'll be back at noon, knocking on these same no doors.
And if again no sales I make,
I'll be back again and again
Until I get some yes doors—
So to pay these bills.
Aha!
You get my drift?

— 17 —

Because of You I'm Me

I have told you many lies and fairy tales, according to you.
But
Know that this isn't one of them.
Believe me when I say you are the best thing that could have ever happened to me.
You are the burning fire that heats up my heart's desire.
You are the driving force to my destination.
You are my weaknesses,
My sadness,
My mistakes.
I often wonder, Without your being in my life,
Who else would I be?
For
I am who I am
All
Because of
You.

—❧ 18 ❧—

I Needed You

I don't want to ever grow up just to understand you,
For you never took the time to shine your light on me.
Now you are trying to redefine who I'm supposed to be?
Man, get out of here!
For the record, with you not in my life, I'm doing just fine, as you can
surely see.

—❧ 19 ❧—

Sailors, Sail On

Sail on, sailors—
Sail on, sail on, sail on and on.
Rock your boat from side to side while it floats.
Be sure to bring surpluses aboard, just in case your boat shall drift,
way out deep in the big blue sea, where there's no dry land near.
This question I must ask you, please: Should your boat sink,
How well can you swim, and how long can you swim?
Sorry for the interruption. As you were, please.
As you can see, I've been swimming well for a very long time,
For my boat wrecked suddenly, when I least expected it.
So sail on, sailors. Sail on. Sail on, sail on and on.
Rock your boat from side to side while it floats.

4

Spicy Slices (Romance, Delicacy)

This chapter I dedicate to some special self-made lovers. These special lovers sure know how to cook up an appetite for loving. So grab your lover, and get under the covers with some chill red wine. Make sure not to get too intoxicated, for by reading this chapter you'll find the slice to be so nice. It'll spice up your love life. It's destined to rekindle your romance, if sober.

1

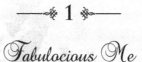

Fabulocious Me

Hey, you!
Are you looking at fabulocious me?
Yes, me. Who else could it be?
So tell me this—is it my fabulocious body that caught your eye?
Or is it my tight, curly locks with the tinted ends, sitting on my head in a modern 'do?

Oh, I'm getting it.

I bet it's my wide hips swinging from side to side while my feet glide my thick thighs.

So …

You are just waiting to see if my big, bubbly boobs are going to jiggle themselves

straight from out of my low-cut striking hot red bra into the palm of desperate hands.

Indeed. Silly me …

So…, it's my bright striking red laced, G-string, underwear that's high above the waist-line of my tight-fitted naive blue jeans, that caught your eyes and had you steering?

All righty, then.

I'll take your word for it. That it's not about any of above I mentioned, and thats it's just all about fabulocious me, and nothing more.

So, tell me,

Will I be just for a night or just for a while, like the others before me?

For fabulocious me …

is looking for a lifetime.

Yeah, baby …

According to my watch, you'll be doing time.

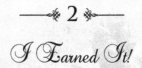

2

I Earned It!

Swam, swam, slam, bam. "Thank you, ma'am."

What was that?

Look, mon, you got pay.

Please, sir, for a little bit more. This time it's on me.

"Okeydoke, if you insist that it's on you."

Swam, swam, swam, swam, swam, swam, slam, slam bam.

"Thank you, ma'am."

Whoa! That was right on … Thank you, sire.
What's that?
Oh no, no, no. Remember I said no pay.
"I insist."
Allrighty, then.
Mercy me, this is much.
You make my day.
Now I can sleep, sleep, sleep the rest of the day.

—❖ 3 ❖—

The Donkey Man Can

Drenched in sweat from my head to toe in the beaming sun on an early
Saturday afternoon,
A Saturday that will forever be the most famous of all Saturdays to me.

Being as tired as tired gets from sweeping up my big backyard,
Filled with fallen dried leaves from my fruit trees.
I decided to finally take a break and sit on my back-door steps.

There I took notice of the fencing that separates my back neighbor
and me.
I could not help but notice an inviting peephole in the rotted wooden
fencing.

So I—yes, I—the "have my man already," got up from off the steps
and took a peek.
Can you imagine what I beheld with my own two eyes?

Well, let's just say "Mercy me" became the language that day,
For mightier than all men this one must be.

Finally I understood the "donkey man" stories that's been going around
The neighborhood and how powerful he can be.

Blessed or cursed are they who have been graced by such a powerful
mightiness,
Which I anxiously waited for my moment of glance, after all the fuss
that's been going on.

Lustfully speaking, as shameful as it may seem, I thought to myself,
Pity or bless is the one beneath, whom he bestowed his trusts upon.

Girls, you know what I mean?
Give me a break.
Goodness mercy, "The donkey man can!"

Manly Girl

I'm a manly girl—it's true.
A manly girl I am.
As bad as it may sound,
No way will one man do.
(There is a Jamaican song that says "I'm a One-Man Girl, A-hah.")
Well, know for certain that's not me,
For one man just won't do.
So if you come across a dozen or more,
Please be kind to send them my way, any time of day,
But never in the mornings after half past ten,
For that is when I prep myself for the many men.
Tell them to bring some wine so we can dine—
That's if they don't mind there will be many of them,
For I'm a manly girl and that's no lie.

5

Thy Eyes

I—yes, flirtatious me—took thy glasses from thy face
and peeked into thy scared, sacred soul.
Thy eyes that my own two eyes are glazing in, without thy eyeglasses on,
are glistening crystal tears of wonders.
Thy eyes are crying for help. *H-e-l-p.*
Help! Thy eyes are crying in disguise to me.
In thy sacred eyes, that thou has opened up to me, all I can see is how
thou wishes to be help and loved by me, as if i'm thy refuge, thy shield,
thy rock, hammer, and hiding place.
Oh powerful, oh magical, oh sweet becomes the night
when thou sneaked on my lips the kiss of a lifetime.
Sweet it is. Yes! Sweeter than a honeycomb and strawberry wine.
However, I dare not sigh for fear thou might take flight because of fright.

6

Dreaming

In the deepness of the night,
While the birdies take their rest,
Thou are deep down in my holiness.
Oh, blessed is thee who maketh thee with such strong hold.
Thou tasteth like honey in milk; no wine compares.
Be willed, by thy grateful mourning and groaning of melody soundings,
Thine engorged gifted weapon, suctioned into thy holiness.
Thus maketh thine to roar as a contented lion after digestion.
Hoops!
I too pray dreams like these never end.

7

Hello

Ring, ring.
Hello, my love, my darling sweetheart, my honey bun, my sugarcane, my la-la-bye.
Are you longing for me as I'm longing for you?
Just close your eyes and listen to the whispers of your heart's desires, and you'll find me near.
I can feel you thrusting your tongue all over my body. Mmmm …
Your strong, muscular arms, drenching my body in oil, mmmm …
My body is shivering by your toxic thrusting.
My body flush-slush in a rush all that's stored up inside.
You're sliding your hands between my slippery, glistening thighs.
Oh, baby, don't stop rubbing what's in between.
Mmmmm, mmmmmm, oh babes! I'm loving it.
Hello?
I can't hear you …
Baby, are you still there?
Hellooo …
Beeeeeeeeeeeeeeeeeeeeeeeeep …

8

Mercy Me!

Sugarcane, sugarcane, can't you see
I'm in love with you?
Sugarcane, sugarcane, come on by—
Come to me in the middle of the night
While I lie sleeping.
Deep down tight, you'll find

My warm embrace waiting for your sugarcane.
Hold me tight.
Make no noise.
I won't bite.
Just have fun
Through the night,
But take your flight before broad daylight.

9

My Red Cherry

My baby got his eyes on my big, red, ripe cherry
Way up high in the top of my cherry tree.
Climb, baby, climb. Climb that tree,
Way up high, where that red cherry lies.
Don't come down from that tree before you pick my red cherry, please.

10

I Like

I like that you like dark-chocolaty me.
I like that you just can't get enough of dark-chocolaty me.
I can feel you swishing me around and about in your mouth,
Daring not to swallow,
For fear of losing my sweet dark-chocolaty flavor.

Lick, lick, licking me all over your lips
Till at last you swallow.
Uhm, a delicious sigh I hear.
Mmm … I admit

I like that you like dark-chocolaty me.
Whoopie-doodle-doo,
I won't ever get over you!

—❧ 11 ❧—

There I lie, on his chest, trying to take a rest,
But he will not rest.
Until he sucks on my two breasts.

—❧ 12 ❧—

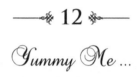

Lick, lick, lick, licking me like a lollipop.
Suck, suck, suck, sucking me like a sugar candy.
Eat, eat, eat, eating me like a gummy bear.
Goodness, gracious, no cooking for me,
For my baby got full from having me.

—❧ 13 ❧—

Blue boy, blue boy,
What's the matter with you?
Come let me blow your big blue horn.

—❧ 14 ❧—

Peter Pan has eaten all the pudding from the pudding pan.
Peter Pan, Peter Pan is licking the pudding pan clean, clean, clean.
Peter Pan, Peter Pan is patting the pan
Which he ate the pudding from.

—❧ 15 ❧—

Truth Be Told

Of course I love you more
Than anything in this word, my dear,
But no way no how will I choose you
Over a sugar candy.

—❧ 16 ❧—

My baby has my back, and that's a fact.
The enemies can't stand that
There'll be raging a war with their hands in the air,
Rocking their waistlines like rock climbers,
Chopping their lips like a Lamborghini.
But none dare to stand up and pick up a stick,
For they know my baby has my back, and that's a fact.
The enemies can't stand that
You have my back.

—❦ 17 ❦—
I Employ Love

Dear friends,

As of today, I promise that as a child of the true Almighty God, and a privileged entrepreneur,
I will *employ love.*
So go ahead and give *love* a try as of today.
You'll find it won't cost you a dime—just some time.

Sincerely,

I Employ Love

—❦ 18 ❦—
I Promise

I promise you a night to take a rest.
I promise you a day to take a break.
I promise you a life to live it well.
I promise all to treat you right.
I promise You, Lord, my soul to keep.
I promise to love, not hate,
To forgive, not retaliate,
To be a giver, not a beggar,
To tell truths, not lies,
To protect the planet, not destroy it,
And
I promise to love my neighbors as myself, no matter their creed, race, and nationality.
And
I promise You, Lord, the Ten Commandments I shall surely keep.

— ❧ 19 ❧ —

One Final Gift

All Jehovah God's creation is created with love and does have the ability
to love.
Life is a gift, not a choice.
What we do with it are the choices we make.
The experiences of life's journey are our embedded story.
So whatever we do, do it well.
Take the time to learn how to love one another, no matter what.
Love is the key to a healthy lifestyle and world peace.

20

My Gratitude

Hello, my friends.
I'm so glad that you came along.
Let's do it again.
Be all that you can be.
Thank you very, very much for all the love, as I love you too.
Know there's no better love than the love Jehovah God has for us.

"Let it rain "Paradontic"
on your loved ones, with
the gift of this first lovely
collectables edition, of
Poetic story telling book.
I thank you, so very
much.
Hugs and kisses.

CPSIA information can be obtained
at www.ICGtesting.com
Printed in the USA
JSHW030511060221
11624JS00001B/25